Nukes to Negotiations

A Path to Peace

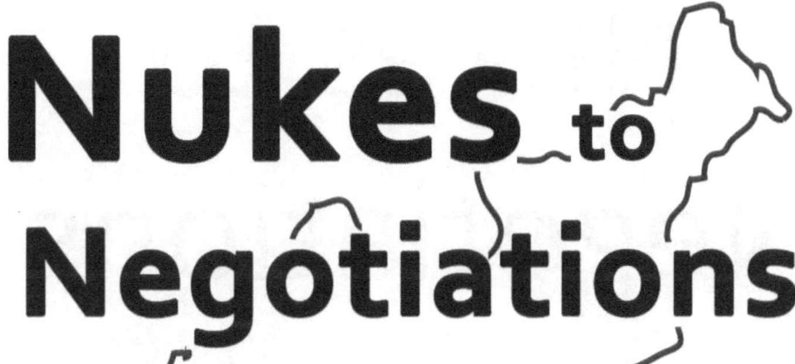

By Katie Evanko-Douglas
CEO of AmeliorMate

Nukes to Negotiations

A Path to Peace

By
Katie Evanko-Douglas

Contact: ameliormate@gmail.com

Published October 23, 2018
Sold by Amazon Digital Services LLC
ASIN: B07HFJQJCT

"The man who says it cannot be done should not interrupt the man doing it."
-Chinese Proverb

This book is dedicated to the Doers.

Preface

The Early Adopters' Edition of this book was written and published mainly as a response to the Trump-Kim Singapore Summit in May of 2018.

It was a book about the doors opened and possibilities afforded by such cooperation between the United States, the Democratic People's Republic of Korea (DPRK), and other regional players. In short, it was a snapshot of where the world stood at that point in time.

Since that initial summit, however, most of the momentum built has come from cooperation between the two Koreas. This cooperation stems from a joint realization of the need to take ownership of the issues affecting their people as well as a joint commitment to solving those problems.

This new and improved "First Edition" is a book about the possibilities afforded by such cooperation, essentially serving as an updated snapshot of where the world stands in October of 2018.

At this moment in time, the following excerpts from the Korea Herald best illustrate why there remains so much cause for optimism:

> *The two Koreas have agreed to break ground for the modernization of cross-border railways and roads in late November or early December, said a statement released by South Korea's Unification Ministry on Monday.*

The statement came as a result of high-level talks held Monday to discuss the implementation of the agreement reached at last month's inter-Korean summit in Pyongyang...

Details on plans to field a united team at the 2020 Olympics and file a bid to jointly host the 2032 Olympics will be discussed at a sports meeting to be held at the recently launched joint liaison office in the border town of Kaesong.

The South and North also shared the view that general-level military talks should be held as soon as possible to push for the establishment of a joint military committee.

Perhaps a Second Edition will focus on a more active and constructive role for the United States in the peace process, for example, if America makes good on its agreement to hold a second Trump-Kim summit and end its "months-long stalemate." Secretary of State Mike Pompeo's recent trip gives a glimmer of hope for such a future.

At the time I am writing this, however, the most notable trend remains how, despite American obstruction, the two Koreas are working together harmoniously and creating real peace with a high-speed rail.

Nukes to Negotiations

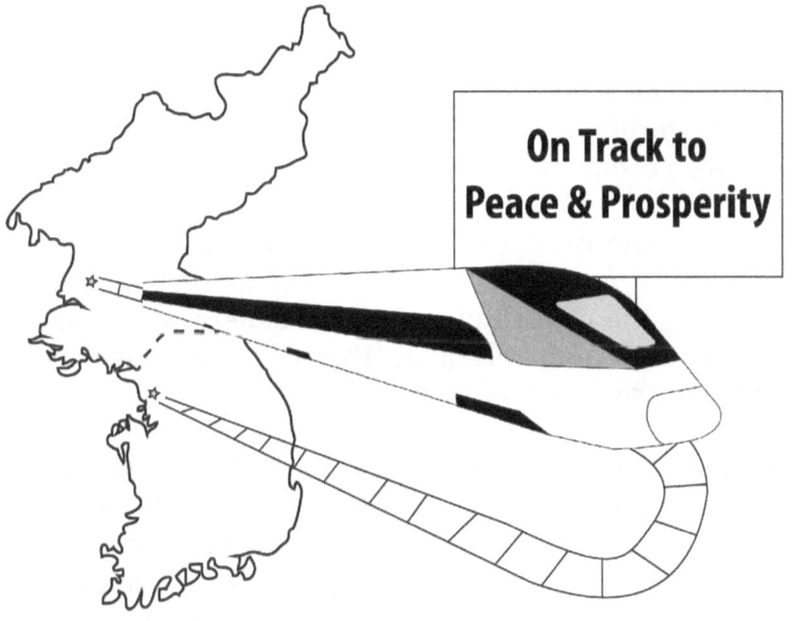

Introduction

Facing the death of the beloved and iconic leader preceding him, he quickly consolidates power.

Though he echoes the hard-line, Cold War-era priorities of his forefathers, he blends them seamlessly with a modern economic agenda.

In the style of a true diplomat, he acknowledges the hardships faced by his people while respecting and praising the contributions of the leaders who founded his nation and raised it through the many great challenges of the Cold War.

Though he has no tolerance for political dissent or challenges to his power, he is poised to open his nation up to the world and invest heavily in the economic and technological future of his people, setting his country on track to become a powerful, modern, global leader.

But this isn't the story of Deng Xiaoping in the 1970's.

It's the story of Kim Jong-un in 2018.

Chapter One

The Vision

Imagine, your plane lands. It's the first time you've visited this East Asian country. You don't know what to expect. Your imagination contains a mix of what you learned about the country growing up and the spectacular reports you've read recently. You brace yourself to be either overwhelmed or underwhelmed.

When you step off the plane, the most modern-looking airport you've ever experienced greets you enthusiastically. You feel like you've stepped into the future. It's so international. You feel like you could be at the UN with the amount of translation AI is doing in the background to make every visitor feel comfortable and understood.

First things first, you need to find your hotel. You expect to be greeted by a taxi driver, most likely a man from the countryside who moved to the city when it started developing rapidly. You mentally prepare yourself to communicate your destination through a language barrier. Imagine your surprise when a driverless car comes to meet you instead.

As you walk toward your ride, you take a deep breath in. Though it's a large and rapidly growing city, the air smells as sweet and clean as the countryside in your home country. The noticeable absence of smog is a remnant of the country's developing with clean energy from the start.

As you make your way to your hotel, you notice what an odd mishmash the city can be. The pace of change and style of infrastructure remind you of China. The level of technology built into the whole smart city feels like Japan. Yet the culture, food, and language are distinctly Korean.

But you didn't visit just to check out the aesthetics and infrastructure. You want to know about the people and the economy that make this country tick. As you walk around the city the next morning, the first thing you notice is how shockingly full of young families it is. Everywhere you look, there are kids going to school or mothers smiling with babies, laughing and chatting with each other in the many green spaces throughout the city.

Though the country had the lowest median age and highest birth rate to begin with, the rapid development of the past decade has produced a predictable yet awe-inspiring youth bulge, pushing the proportion of the population under the age of 25 from just over one-third to just over one-half. It's quite the boon to a region known for its demographic struggle against free-falling birth rates.

The generation now entering the workforce is not only the largest generation in this country's history. It is also the most educated, optimistic, and passionate cohort. Education has always been an important value in this region's culture, but it's still overwhelming to observe such a huge and rapidly growing young workforce wherein every student is taught enough programming to be able to work in the country's dominant industry, cyber-security, or the global technology sector in general right out of high school.

It's a startup founder's dream come true, the most modern city in the world, with a relatively low cost of living, and a large and growing workforce of highly skilled programmers. It's no wonder it's fast becoming one of the hottest startup hubs of the 21st century.

Welcome to Pyongyang 2035.

How is this possible?

I learned most of what I know about innovative thinking and startups alike from Peter Thiel. He begins his book *Zero to One* with a favorite interview question.

"What important truth do very few people agree with you on?"

He describes the question as "intellectually difficult because the knowledge that everyone is taught in school is by definition agreed upon. And it's psychologically difficult because anyone trying to answer must say something she knows to be unpopular."

I know such a future is possible because of one such truth; **The world is incredibly lucky to have Kim Jong-Un leading North Korea because he is a capable and visionary leader who genuinely cares about the wellbeing of his people.**

This is not meant to discount the contributions of South Korean President Moon Jae-in. It is to point out that they are not nearly as controversial in the West. As an ally to the United States, he is not demonized. It is assumed he wants to do what is best for his people. And because he ran and was elected on a platform of improving relations with North Korea, it is not surprising that he is able to make such important contributions. It is therefore common knowledge and popular to admit that Moon Jae-in is an important half of the puzzle who is doing extraordinary things.

"Common knowledge" on the character, motivations, and capabilities of Kim Jong-Un, on the other hand, are mostly incorrect in the West and the truth is extremely unpopular. I know in publishing this book I will continue to be attacked for supporting a "murderous dictator" who enjoys starving people, for working against the interests of the United States in a zero-sum game, and for contributing to a global trend of millennials making Western democracy a thing of the past via negligence and ignorance.

But if I can help prevent the chaos and utter destruction of a nuclear war, a worldwide cyber war more destructive than any conventional world war thus far in human history, or failed state scenario, all while helping to increase the wellbeing of millions of humans and restoring a semblance of stability to our international political and financial systems, enduring such attacks on my intellect and character will be well worth it.

The reason I see Kim Jong-Un differently than most likely stems from my academic background. I spent much of my time as an undergraduate studying the history of East Asia, especially Chinese politics and the economic development of the region in general. Most people look at Kim Jong-Un and apply the same caricatures they've been applying to his father and his grandfather for decades.

But I look at him and see behavioral patterns similar to a different regional leader, as was alluded to in the introduction. That leader is China's Deng Xiaoping.

To put it simply, Encyclopedia Britannica describes Deng Xiaoping as "the most powerful figure in the People's Republic of China from the late 1970s until his death in 1997. He abandoned many orthodox communist doctrines and attempted to incorporate elements of the free-enterprise system and other reforms into the Chinese economy.

Deng restored China to domestic stability and economic growth after the disastrous excesses of the Cultural Revolution. Under his leadership, China acquired a rapidly growing economy, rising standards of living, considerably expanded personal and cultural freedoms, and growing ties to the world economy. Deng also left in place a mildly authoritarian government that remained committed to the CCP's one-party rule even while it relied on free-market mechanisms to transform China into a developed country."

He is in many ways the father of modern China, lifting millions from poverty and creating the economic powerhouse we see today through sheer force of will.

I see a similar drive in Kim Jong-Un.

Three-Pronged Approach to
North Korean Development

There are a few basic planks of development North Korea, like any country, will have to focus on in the beginning. These include developing manufacturing jobs for low-skilled labor as well as agriculture, healthcare, and education systems.

These are areas even the United States should focus on developing further. Every country needs them. This book is not meant to bore you explaining the obvious.

This book is meant to highlight North Korea's unique elements that make it possible to create the unique vision for the future described earlier in this chapter.

The rest of this chapter is dedicated to describing a three-pronged approach specific to and built upon the vision and values of North Korean leadership both past and present: cyber-security dominance.

The Three Prongs

1. Establish a state-owned enterprise focused on cyber-security.
2. Build high-tech infrastructure utilizing renewable energy.
3. Invest in universal education with a strong emphasis on 21st century skills such as programming and software engineering.

Let's explore each step in more detail as, rather than standing alone, they build on each other, compounding the effects of the previous step in order to grow to the magnificent vision described earlier.

Prong One
State-Owned Enterprise

The first step is to establish a state-owned enterprise focused on cyber-security. The logic behind this is simple; North Korea's dominant industry currently appears to be employing Black Hat hackers to find ways of making money to feed the people in the face of tough sanctions. This is made possible by intense, long-term investments the government has been making for decades in preparation for a global shift to predominantly cyber warfare.

The New York Times describes North Korea as employing an army of over 6,000 hackers, which is able to generate at least hundreds of millions if not over a billion dollars annually.

In order to turn their intense, and quite prescient, investments of the past couple decades (identifying and training thousands of hackers) into a legitimate state-owned enterprise, North Korea simply has to shift that labor to White Hat hacking.

It would be like if a team of the most skilled bank robbers went from making money exploiting banks' vulnerabilities to rob them, to making money exploiting banks' vulnerabilities to inform the banks of how they can best fix their problems and protect themselves from bank robbers.

That's a legitimate, scalable business the banking industry as a whole would be lucky to have access to. If the world's most skilled bank robbers are the ones protecting your bank, the world's second-most skilled bank robbers are highly unlikely to ever break in. What bank wouldn't want access to that sort of peace of mind?

The clearest explanation I've seen of the importance of both Black and White Hat hackers in our species' future comes from Episode 32 of Crash Course's Computer Science series, Hackers & Cyber Attacks:

> Despite all of the hard-working White Hats, exploits documented online, and software engineering best practices, **cyber attacks happen on a daily basis. They cost the global economy roughly half a trillion dollars annually. And that figure will only increase** as we become more reliant on computing systems.
>
> This is especially worrying to governments as infrastructure is increasingly computer-driven, like power plants, the electrical grid, traffic lights, water treatment plants, oil refineries, air traffic control, and lots of other key systems.
>
> Many experts predict that **the next major war will be fought in cyberspace, where nations are brought to their knees not by physical attack but rather crippled economically and infrastructurally** through cyber warfare.

There may not be any bullets fired, but **the potential for lives lost is still very high, maybe even higher than conventional warfare.**

Cyber-security is multi-billion dollar, growing field with an acute shortage of skilled labor. It's lucky for North Korea there happens to be a huge pain point in the field they happen to be amazing at. This is the perfect point in time for North Korea to establish a legitimate state-owned enterprise focusing on cyber-security.

Forbes expects the cyber-security market to reach $170 billion by 2020. That's up from just $75 billion as recently as 2015. Any entrepreneur knows, gaining even a small share of a market that large with such rapid growth is a recipe for financial success. If North Korea could establish a state-owned enterprise that captured just 1.2% of the global market, they would double their annual revenue compared to the Black Hat hacking status quo.

It would also benefit many countries' defense and intelligence units because North Korea could help them defend their countries against Russian hackers, for example. Peter Thiel advises starting with a small niche. One niche that might be a natural fit for North Korea is threat intelligence which itself has a compound annual growth rate of 10%.

I hypothesize that by creating such a state-owned enterprise, North Korea would generate billions of dollars in revenue annually. This would give them ample capital to invest in the next two prongs of their development. It would give them increased autonomy as well because they would have more leverage than the average country when negotiating deals for development loans. They would have the freedom to walk away from deals that don't best suit the needs of their people, which brings us to the second prong.

Prong Two
Infrastructure

Now that we know how North Korea can quickly develop its first industry specialization, let's look at how to invest those profits for further growth.

Being a late bloomer is not always a bad thing. Sometimes it has huge benefits. For example, if you're developing after your neighbors, you can pull on their expertise and skip many traditional steps. It actually allows you to be more modern than countries that developed earlier on in their histories.

Here are some examples of playing the late bloomer card in the global development game:

- Skip landline telephones. Go straight to mobile smart phones.
- Skip smog. Go straight to clean, renewable energy.
- Skip dial-up. Go straight to high-speed fiber.

The list goes on but basically, late bloomers can optimize from the beginning for many of the technological transitions traditionally developed countries struggle with and sometimes find insurmountable at scale. By adopting cutting-edge technology from the beginning of their development cycles, they are essentially able to "leap-frog" ahead of many traditionally developed countries.

Technology is developing so rapidly, it is impossible to predict exactly what the end result will be. You've heard of smart cities, but this will be a whole smart country with the chance to design itself almost from scratch.

It will be the most technologically advanced development project in human history. It will synthesize all the lessons South Korea, China, and Japan learned during the development of their infrastructure to make the smartest and most effective infrastructure in the world.

I personally find the prospect of such a project incredibly exciting.

Prong Three
Education

Education is another example where North Korea may well be able to "leap-frog" over many traditionally developed countries. Though they already have an education system capable of picking out the best and the brightest and pushing them to fulfill their full potential as hackers, they will have a unique opportunity to re-design their education system almost from scratch if they choose to.

This means that instead of trying to painstakingly alter a legacy system created during the industrial revolution, they can use modern technology to create a system that caters to the actual way humans learn best, finding the unique strengths of every child and developing them while including 21st century skills like programming and software engineering as a core part of the children's curriculum.

This way, they can quickly create the most desirable young workforce of the 21st century and make North Korea the hottest startup hub in the world.

Chapter Two

The Methods

By this point you may be asking, who is this author, why is she qualified to make such recommendations, and how in the world did she come up with them?

In short, I'm simply a young professional, classically trained as a diplomat with a focus on Asian development from the University of Nebraska-Lincoln.

Apparently, I possess just enough inexperience to have the audacity to suggest we go back to basics and use the principles of international negotiations we all [should have] learned in international negotiations 101.

A First Principles Approach

Though it wasn't described with this exact terminology, my college courses basically taught me to conduct international negotiations from first principles. That is, you break down what each party wants to its simplest terms then find creative ways to combine everyone's end games.

It's not unlike the approach Elon Musk takes when building battery packs. Instead of thinking, battery packs have historically been too expensive to be feasible to produce at scale, he thought:

What are the components that go into battery packs? Can we find more efficient ways to put those components together?

The answer turned out to be yes, ushering in a revolution in sustainable energy.

He thinks from first principles to solve technology and business problems using STEM fields because that's what he's trained in. I think from first principles to solve public policy and diplomacy problems using SBS fields because that's what I'm trained in.

In this case, instead of asking about the components of a battery pack, I asked, what are the components of a successful nuclear treaty with North Korea? Can we find more efficient ways to put those components together?

I believe the answer is a resounding yes. But before we dive deeper into the "how" of things, let's examine how exactly we generate the "what."

The two basic steps to this process include:

1. Figure out *what each party wants.*
2. Figure out how to *combine said desires* into a mutually beneficial end game.

It's easier said than done for sure, but **it is not impossible.**

What Does Everyone Want?

The first step of this approach is to identify what all parties want most. These are my educated guesses based on a decade spent studying the region:

- **North Korea**: For Kim Jong-un to stay in power while making a lot of money to pour into development
- **South Korea**: To not be at war with a country they consider more family than enemy, and to have the assurance of lasting peace and stability
- **China**: Stability, a lack of refugees from either a nuclear war or a regime collapse/failed state scenario
- **Japan**: To be involved enough to make sure there is absolutely no chance their country will experience the devastation of nuclear weapons ever again
- **United States**: For North Korea to not have any nuclear weapons capabilities

The second step is to figure out an end game that synthesizes everyone's desires seamlessly and gets everyone excited enough to follow through on the tough work of negotiating and implementing an appropriate treaty.

The vision should include the "what" of each party's individual end games while reminding everyone "why" the negotiations are so important.

The end game created by this method was the vision described in chapter one.

Chapter Three

The Mechanics

While having a vision and knowing "what" needs done is an important first step, it's mostly wishful thinking until accompanied by the "how." The final chapter of this book is dedicated to giving an overview of exactly how North Korea can achieve such a future. It is not quick and it is not necessarily easy, but it is well worthwhile.

My preliminary, 5-step plan for implementing the aforementioned methodology is as follows:

1. **Form a regional organization** in charge of doing the work of drafting a treaty.
2. **Create a vision** for a beautiful future for North Korea and the region.
3. **Identify the resources** needed to achieve said vision.
4. **Draft a treaty** which details said resources and exchanges them for nuclear weapons capabilities.
5. **Sign and ratify.**

Step One
Form a Regional Organization

The first step is to figure out who is responsible for the nitty-gritty work of drafting a nuclear disarmament treaty. Though the Trump-Kim Summit was a good first step in building trust and getting the ball rolling, it did not include a comprehensive, legally binding treaty. It didn't provide a clear enough framework to achieve the vision laid out in chapter one.

And that's okay. That wasn't the point of that particular summit. Drafting an actual treaty is something that takes a lot more work behind the scenes than a summit with a resolution does. Something this big and complex takes time, especially if you want to do it right and avoid future complications.

I recommend forming a regional organization to handle this nitty-gritty work because it's the most efficient path I can think of. Such a path is allowed under Chapter VIII of the Charter of the United Nations.

The regional organization would consist of the Democratic People's Republic of Korea (DPRK), the Republic of Korea, the People's Republic of China (PRC), and Japan.

The organization would work with the UN Security Council Sanctions Committee on North Korea, which is allowed to make legally binding decisions on the matter, to draft an excellent treaty.

I believe this approach makes sense because it allows the most affected countries to take ownership of the situation and work as a team, encouraging them to build trust and iron out any disagreements privately before presenting a draft of a treaty to the public or the committee.

It cuts down on confusion about who is responsible for making this treaty happen. It basically delegates the work to specific parties who can then roll up their sleeves, put their heads down, and focus solely on producing the best treaty of the 21st century.

This regional organization would be allowed to include other countries if it wished to and would be allowed to work with allies, such as the United States, if it so desired.

Step Two
Create a Vision

While I presented one possible vision for North Korea in the first chapter of this book, only a vision created by talking extensively to affected leaders while exploring all the possibilities afforded by modern technology and infrastructure would be complete.

The vision in this book is a good starting point as it shows some of the amazing possibilities available.

But it will ultimately be up to the regional organization to create a comprehensive and detailed vision and it will be up to Kim Jong-un to approve said vision.

Step Three
Identify the Resources

Oftentimes, past negotiations with North Korea and other countries haven't been effective because they were too one-sided. Parties wanted to "win" and look strong rather than achieve any specific, sustainable end game.

They treated negotiations like the zero-sum game they aren't.

Going back to the basics means treating each party with respect and the expectation they are a rational actor who is simply doing their best to do right by their people.

Under this approach, one would recognize that giving up nuclear weapons capabilities means giving up a lot of leverage. It's a big ask. A rational leader would not make such a trade without receiving something of equal or greater value in return.

This step is basically just laying out the specific resources required to achieve the mutually agreed upon vision for a great future for North Korea, the region, and the world.

Only when those resources are identified and clearly laid out can they be put into a treaty. You can't write a treaty that says if you give up your nuclear capabilities, you can have a great future in 15 years. It's too vague. It's not a fair trade.

Once everyone agrees on what success would look like, technical experts can be hired to lay out the specific things needed for success. For example, $X in development loans, $Y in aid, Z technical expertise from surrounding countries, etc.

As a rational actor, there's no way Kim Jong-un would agree to sign a treaty without the benefits clearly outweighing the costs. Step three is the moment all the components of a successful treaty, the costs and benefits, are clearly laid out, negotiated, and agreed upon in an informal setting within the regional organization.

Step Four
Draft a Treaty

Receiving the capability to achieve the aforementioned vision of the future, where North Korea becomes a highly developed, powerful, and indispensible nation within the global cyber-security ecosystem, is of greater value than nuclear weapons capabilities.

But just like one side requires specifics and guarantees on nuclear disarmament and verification, Kim Jong-un should require specifics and guarantees regarding the resources needed to create his desired end game for his country.

So if Japan is offering to pay for the International Atomic Energy Agency inspections, it needs to be included in a legally binding treaty.

If any countries or development banks are offering loans for infrastructure development at an extremely competitive interest rate, it needs to be included in a legally binding treaty.

If any governments want to hire North Korea's newly created state-owned enterprise for threat intelligence work, and North Korea is counting on that money to fulfill their development budget, it needs to be included in a legally binding treaty.

This step will also include working with the committee to make sure it covers all relevant bases under international law and fully solves the issues at hand in a sustainable and permanent way.

Step four is the moment all the components of a successful treaty are clearly laid out, negotiated, and agreed upon in a formal way with actors both within and outside the regional organization to draft a legally binding document.

Step Five
Sign and Ratify

Step five is fairly self-explanatory. Once the treaty has been written and all relevant parties have agreed upon a final version, it is ready to be signed and ratified by all relevant countries.

Only then does it become legally binding, allowing us to move forward full-steam ahead and build a glorious future.

That is the final step of this how-to manual.

Conclusion

The DPRK hit a crossroads following the success of the Trump-Kim Summit of 2018.

Down one path lies the traditional, continued isolation likely ending in nuclear war and/or eventual failed state scenario.

Down the other path lies the modern, economic and technological development ending in the creation of one of the most innovative and powerful countries of the 21st century.

The second path is difficult. It requires a tremendous amount of courage and elbow grease from the entire region. I believe it is well worth the effort, but it's not up to me.

And it's not up to you. It's not up to the United States, or China, or South Korea, or Japan, or any other country or individual.

It's up to Kim Jong-un and his vision for his people.

I remain optimistic.

References

Buckland, K., & Urabe, E. (2018, June 16). Abe Says Trump-Kim Summit Built Foundation for Denuclearization. Retrieved October 17, 2018, from https://www.bloomberg.com/news/articles/2018-06-16/abe-says-trump-kim-summit-built-foundation-for-denuclearization

Crash Course. (2017, October 18). Hackers & Cyber Attacks: Crash Course Computer Science #32. Retrieved October 17, 2018, from https://www.youtube.com/watch?v=_GzE99AmAQU

Editors of Encyclopaedia Britannica. (2018, September 21). Deng Xiaoping. Retrieved October 17, 2018, from https://www.britannica.com/biography/Deng-Xiaoping

Kim Jong Un's 2018 New Year's Address. (2018, January 01). Retrieved October 17, 2018, from https://www.ncnk.org/node/1427

Min-kyung, J. (2018, October 15). [Breaking] Koreas agree to start railway, road work by Dec. Retrieved October 17, 2018, from http://www.koreaherald.com/view.php?ud=20181015000711

Morgan, S. (2015, December 21). Cybersecurity Market
        Reaches $75 Billion In 2015; Expected To Reach
        $170 Billion By 2020. Retrieved October 18,
        2018, from
        https://www.forbes.com/sites/stevemorgan/20
        15/12/20/cybersecurity-market-reaches-75-
        billion-in-2015-expected-to-reach-170-billion-
        by-2020/#476b6c2930d6

Rose, K. (2012, September 07). Foundation 20 // Elon
        Musk. Retrieved October 18, 2018, from
        https://www.youtube.com/watch?v=L-
        s_3b5fRd8

Sanger, D. E., Kirkpatrick, D., & Perlroth, N. (2017,
        October 15). The World Once Laughed at North
        Korean Cyberpower. No More. Retrieved October
        18, 2018, from
        https://www.nytimes.com/2017/10/15/world/
        asia/north-korea-hacking-cyber-sony.html

Thiel, P., & Masters, B. (2014). *Zero to one notes on
        startups, or how to build the future.* New York,
        NY: Crown Business.

United Nations, Charter of the United Nations, 24
        October 1945, 1 UNTS XVI, available at:
        http://www.refworld.org/docid/3ae6b3930.ht
        ml [accessed 17 October 2018]

About the Author

Katie Evanko-Douglas holds a B.A. in Global Studies and Political Science from the University of Nebraska-Lincoln. During her undergraduate career, she specialized in development in East and South Asia as well as researching women and governance.

She is also the CEO/Founder of AmeliorMate, a consulting and software startup that **believes humans matter most**.

AmeliorMate does work consulting with governments on international negotiations and development to make sure they're able to achieve the highest level of wellbeing possible for their people while building tools for social and behavior scientists so the wellbeing of human populations in general can be more easily measured and objectively improved.

Contact: ameliormate@gmail.com